Take A Winter Nature Walk

By Jane Kirkland
Edited by
Rob Kirkland
Dorothy Burke
Melanie Palaisa

You're about to set out on a real adventure. Not only will you make discoveries and see things you haven't noticed before, you're going to complete this unfinished book—and only you can finish it! You are going to take a winter nature walk and discover nature and the many surprises it holds.

One of my favorite winter nature discoveries happened to me when I wasn't even interested in nature and it happened in an unusual place—my grocery store parking lot!

It was a chilly winter day. I had just finished my shopping and was loading my groceries into the back of my van. I reached up to close the back door and there, above my head, I saw a Bald Eagle.

It was soaring in circles. I gasped at the sight. I couldn't believe my eyes! A Bald Eagle—right there in the sky above my neighborhood! WOW!

I rushed to the state park next to my house to tell the rangers about my exciting discovery. But the rangers weren't excited—or surprised.

I'll never forget that Bald Eagle as long as I live! If I didn't see it, I would have never written this book. If I didn't write this book, you couldn't read this book. If you didn't read this book, you and I would never have met and we would have never discovered nature together. Hey! That Bald Eagle changed my life—and yours, too.

What Was I Thinking?

Before I wrote Take a Walk® books, I wrote more than 40 books about computer software. I spent my life at my desk, in front of the computer, day in and day out. When I started to take nature breaks every day, my life changed! I discovered and fell in love with nature. And now, years later, I still see new things every day.

One ranger said, "Jane, Bald Eagles have been soaring over this neighborhood for twenty years. They visit mostly in the winter because a part of our lake is so deep it doesn't freeze over like the other nearby lakes. They come for the food—the fish and the waterfowl. I'm surprised you haven't seen one before".

It was exciting to see the Bald Eagle. But it was a shock to learn that Bald Eagles had been around my neighborhood for a long time and I was too busy doing other things to notice. I made a promise to myself that day that I would take a nature break every day—and look to the sky, at the ground, and all around me, just to notice what's nearby and what's happening in nature. I'm so glad I made that promise!

Are you ready to explore nature in the winter? Are you ready to see what you've been missing? This book will help you to learn how to find and safely observe nature.

There are three sections to this book: *Ready, Set,* and *Go!* Here in the *Ready* section you'll learn how to prepare for your winter nature walk.

In the *Set* section, I'll explain why some birds leave for the winter and why some animals sleep. You'll learn about the advantages of white fur and white feathers.

In the *Go* section you'll learn how to find and identify animals and the tracks they leave in the snow. This section also contains a page for you to take field notes, one to draw a map, and another to record your observations. There are even photos to help you identify the wildlife you find.

Throughout this book you'll see artwork and poetry by other kids—just like you—and fun and interesting sidebars. You can read this book in any order you wish. Just remember it isn't finished until you go outside to explore.

Let it snow! Winter days are short and there might not be enough daylight for a nature walk after school. But snow days are perfect for nature walks. So are weekends when you can take friends or family with you. Maybe you'll see wildlife sharing with their friends, too, like this Northern Cardinal and White-throated Sparrow.

Once you know where to look and what to look for, you'll see just how exciting a winter nature walk can be! There is nature around us, above us, and under our feet all year long. Nature is everywhere and to see it you only need to look! Are you ready to discover nature in winter?

Be Prepared

Dress properly. Wear shoes that will keep your feet warm and dry. Wear layers of clothing because layering is good insulation and if you get too warm, you can remove an outer layer to cool off. A hat will not only keep your head warm. It will help to keep your body warm too because heat escapes through our heads. Wear gloves or mittens, too. Face it, if you're too cold, your feet are wet, or your hands hurt from the cold, you won't enjoy being outdoors. But dressing properly can help you to tolerate winter weather much more comfortably.

Take this book. This book will help you to find and observe nature.

Leave only footprints. The only thing you should leave behind you is your footprints in the snow.

What Can You See Below?

Look at the winter scene below, painted by my friend Bradley Smith. See if you can find a groundhog, a deer, three Chickadees, and two Cardinals. Look carefully and you can even see a butterfly! The Mourning Cloak butterfly is one of the few butterflies that winters over in cold areas as an adult! It is in the pile of dirt and leaves.

Winter

Winter is everywhere.
Ice covers the water.
Nights are long and cold.
Tracks of animals as they go.
Evergreens covered with snow.
Resting for spring.

By Ryan Evanko, age 11,
Port Matilda, PA.

Winter is cool! Seriously. I realize that some people think that winter is a slow and boring time of year. They are simply uninformed. Sure, the days are short—and cold. But that's because the earth is tilted on its axis. In the winter months North America is tilted away from the sun and we have fewer hours of sunlight. In fact, in winter we experience the shortest day of our year (see the sidebar, right).

The short, cold days are exactly what make winter exciting. They set the scene for a life or death battle for plants and animals. Because there is less sunlight, everything gets colder. Less sunlight and colder temperatures mean plants can't grow as fast.

Cold-blooded animals, such as worms, insects, amphibians, and reptiles, can't move around as fast. Warm-blooded animals, such as birds and mammals, have to work harder to stay warm.

If the temperature gets cold enough for water to freeze, living things are in great danger of dying. Plants and animals have water inside them. If the water inside their cells freezes, those cells will die. If enough cells die, the whole plant or animal may die. So plants and animals have many ways of surviving winter weather.

4

Plants have three ways of surviving cold. One: produce a lot of seeds, then die (like sunflowers). The seeds survive the winter and sprout in the spring.

Two: die back to the root system (like tulips, which have bulbs). The roots survive the winter underground and sprout in the spring.

And three: reduce the amount of water in their cells (like trees and shrubs). The water between the cells may freeze, but the cells, with hardly any water in them, won't freeze. In spring, when the ice between the cells melts, the cells absorb the water again.

Animals have five ways of surviving winter. One: lay eggs and die. Two: find a warm place and sleep. Three: reduce the water in their cells (like plants do). Four: leave—go someplace else for the winter. And five (which only the warm-blooded animals can do): stay active and tough it out. Some frogs go underground. Some bats sleep. Some butterflies lay eggs. Some birds fly south. Some squirrels rob bird feeders all winter long. ☺

Winter is not a slow and boring time in nature—it's exciting! Nature in the winter is beautiful—and totally cool!

Sunrise, Sunset

The shortest day of the year in North America happens in December and is called the winter solstice (SOUL-stiss). On that day there are about 10 hours of daylight in the southern U.S., 9 hours in the northern U.S., and 6 in Alaska.

The longest day of the year is in June and it's called the summer solstice. On that day there are about 14 hours of daylight in the southern U.S., 15 in the northern U.S., and 19 in Alaska.

One day each spring and fall, daylight and darkness both last about 12 hours everywhere. Those days are known as the vernal (spring) and autumnal (fall) equinoxes (EE-kwuh-nok-ses).

See some good earth orbit animations on the Web by searching for "animation earth sun".

New Words?

Dormant
(DOOR-ment)

Asleep or inactive. In a state of rest.

Uber
(OO-ber)

The ultimate, most powerful, and best.

From the German word über.

Riddle

I remember this riddle from when I was about six years old. I still think it's clever. Ready? Who brings toys to bears at Christmas? See the answer below.

Santa Clawsl

Different animals do different things to survive the winter. Some sleep, some move away, and others stay and winter over. Those that sleep are *dormant*; their hearts, breathing, and brain activity slow down.

Perhaps the most famous winter sleepers are the bears. And here's a secret: bears don't *hibernate* (HIGH-ber-nate), not exactly. Bears enter a state of *torpor* (TOR-por) in the winter. You and I use the word "hibernate" to mean winter sleep. But there are different kinds of winter sleep for animals. One of those kinds of sleep is torpor.

During torpor, an animal's body temperature drops slightly and its heart rate and breathing slow down. But it can be easily awakened. Some animals enter a state of torpor for days or weeks, some just during very cold nights. Torpor is a kind of light hibernation. And hibernation is a sort of *uber* torpor!

During true hibernation, the body temperature, heartbeat, and breathing drop to a near-death state. Animals live off their body fat. It takes about 18 hours for an animal to enter a state of hibernation and about 3 hours for it to wake up. Most hibernators are mid-sized mammals and rodents.

Unlike bears, hibernating animals won't awaken if you walk near them or make noises. In fact, hibernating animals won't wake up until it is time for them to wake up. Bats, woodchucks, and some ground squirrels hibernate.

Bears are cute, that's for sure. Bears are dangerous, too. Stay away from bears and bear dens at all times. Remember, they can awaken from their winter torpor if you disturb them.

A Prairie Dog is a kind of ground squirrel and a true hibernator. This guy is awake so it must be spring!

Rabbits don't hibernate in the winter but they are less active to conserve energy. Drawing by Aliya Williams, age 10, of Moorestown, NJ.

...Some Serious Winter Sleepers

Reptiles and amphibians have a state of long-term sleep, too. They are cold blooded animals and their body temperature drops as it gets colder outside. To survive the cold, they enter a state similar to hibernation called *brumation* (brew-MAY-shun). Some brumate under water. Others gather close together in burrows, in caves, under leaves, or between rocks to help keep their dormant bodies from freezing. The gathering place is called a *hibernaculum* (high-ber-NAK-you-lum).

Some insects become dormant by entering a state called diapause (DIE-a-paws). In diapause all growth stops, allowing insects to overwinter as larvae or eggs, as in the case of butterflies and dragonflies. Diapause is triggered by days becoming shorter, temperatures lower, or changes in the quantity or quality of food. Diapause can occur at times other than winter.

Hibernation, torpor, diapause, and brumation are all states of dormancy and all ways to survive the winter. Sometimes I feel dormant. If the weather is too cold or wet to comfortably take a nature walk, I stay cuddled up by the fireplace in my pj's and watch the birds at my feeder outside. That counts as my official nature break for the day. Why not? Observing nature should be fun—you don't have to freeze to do it.

This Red-sided Garter Snake is lying on a bed of leaves in late autumn. One spring, I found about 15 garter snakeskins in an opened bag of mulch I had stored in my garage over the winter. I'm sure glad I didn't find 15 snakes!

If, during your winter nature walk, you come across a dormant animal, don't disturb it. Also keep your eyes open for animals that have awakened for a short time to find food—such as this cute little chipmunk.

More Wintering Animals

Fish survive winter by moving into deeper water that (hopefully) won't freeze. Raccoons and skunks enter a state of torpor during the coldest of the winter weather. Chipmunks sleep a lot but come up from their dens for food during the winter. Beavers stay in their lodges but come out for food they store nearby. Squirrels often build nests in tree trunks and stay inside a lot to keep warm. Turtles and frogs burrow into the mud and go to sleep. I spend a lot of time in my office but emerge to take a nature walk when the sun shines or the snow falls!

Butterflies in Winter?

The Mourning Cloak Butterfly winters over as an adult butterfly, buried under leaves, in tree holes, or under loose bark on a tree trunk. On sunny, warm February days it might awaken and fly for a few hours. A butterfly in winter. Who knew?

This raccoon has awakened from his winter sleep just long enough to be drawn by Victoria Geyer, age 12, of Cinnaminson, NJ.

New Word?

Species (SPEE-shees):

A certain kind, variety, or type of living creature.

Birds in Winter

*Eating more food
Eating more often
Footprints in the snow
Duller colors
Weather predictors
Fluffed up feathers
Beautiful*

*By Kelsey Leach, age 7,
of Menomonie, WI.*

Different animals do different things to survive the winter. Some sleep, some move away, and others stay and winter over. Those that move away *migrate*—which means they move with the seasons to follow their food source.

Caribou, whales, and some butterflies, dragonflies, and even bats migrate. Animals often migrate in very large groups and sometimes mixed **species** travel together. There is safety in numbers. There are also more pairs of eyes to look for food and spot predators.

Migrating birds head south in the autumn to their winter grounds and north in the spring to their breeding grounds. Some people don't realize that their backyards are the wintering grounds for species that nest farther north of them.

I live in Southeast Pennsylvania. The Dark-eyed Junco is a species of bird that winters here. I see them at my feeders as I look out my office window every winter. When they arrive, I know winter has arrived.

Follow that food! Many species of birds migrate and several species of blackbirds, including the Yellow-headed Blackbird, travel in large, mixed flocks. In large groups, there are more eyes to find food and more defenders against predators.

Dark-eyed Juncos are called "snowbirds" because they visit our area just for the winter. Their Latin name is Junco Hyemalis, which comes from the Latin word for winter—hyemal.

Red-tailed Hawks in northern areas (Alaska, Canada, northern United States) mostly migrate. But some with established territories might winter over. Drawing by Courtney Moore, age 9, of Vestal, NY.

Animals that migrate have a difficult fight for survival—especially the birds. It is estimated that only 30 percent of wild birds survive their first migration. Weather plays a big factor in migration survival. So do cars, people, cell towers, hi-rises, housing developments, pollution, and habitat and native plant destruction.

Animals need to eat, drink, and rest along their migratory paths and every year that becomes more and more difficult for them. As we continue to strip our landscape, we remove food sources and shelter for animals. Our highways make it difficult for animals to cross without crashing into windshields or getting run over. We destroy our natural world faster than animals can adapt to the changes we make. Many species of plants and animals are going extinct because of loss of habitat.

We can help. Even the small things we do can make a difference. We can supply food by hanging feeders and planting native plants. We can provide water sources. We can be aware of the animals that migrate and the seasons in which they move and keep a protective eye and ear out for them. These things will help the animals that migrate and those that winter over too.

One of my favorite migration moments happens every year at a wildlife management area about an hour's drive from my home. Tens of thousands of Snow Geese, migrating north, stop over to feed and rest for a week or two. I've seen as many as 120,000 snow geese at one time. It may look it but, they are not all in this photo.

Where I live some Eastern Bluebirds migrate south for the winter but others stay. Every year I feed mealworms to the wintering Bluebirds. Sometimes I see as many as 10 birds crowded on the table to get at the food.

Alaska to New Zealand

Some species of birds travel thousands of miles every year to and from their nesting and winter territories. In 2007, scientists tracked a female Bar-tailed Godwit (a shorebird) that flew 7,145 miles (11,500 kilometers) from Alaska to New Zealand. It never stopped to take a break for food or drink. That was the longest migration ever measured. WOW. I once flew to New Zealand—in a plane, of course—and it took 12 hours. I ate, drank, slept, and watched two movies. I also complained about the long flight. What a wuss!

Winter

Winter wind is whirling.
Snowflakes are swirling.
Squirrels settle in their nests.
Birds fly south for the winter.
Bears hibernate in their caves.
Trees lose leaves.
The grass is covered with snow.
Winter is here!

By Anna Mullane, age 7,
of N. Chelmsford, MA.

Swallowed by Swallows!

One fall day I was taking a walk in Cape May NJ. The path where I walked was lined with Bayberry bushes. Suddenly, hundreds (maybe thousands) of migrating Tree Swallows swooped down from the sky into the bushes. In about five minutes flat they stripped those bushes of all the berries. What a sight that was!

Get Set! Meet...

Adaptations (a-dap-TAY-shens)

Changes that a species makes to help it survive when its environment, food source, or world changes. Adaptations take place over many generations.

A Favorite

This is one of my favorite books about nature in the winter. It is a short story about a snowman and the real wildlife that curiously checks him out, shown with beautiful photographs.

Stranger in the Woods

By Carl R. Sams and Jean Stoik. Published by EDCO Publishing.

Deer by Remy Ryan, age 12, of Rockville, MD.

Some species of animals stay active all winter long. To survive they have developed **adaptations** that help them to find food and stay warm.

Food can be scarce in the winter. Some animals adapt to winter's lack of food by changing their diet. Some store food for the winter. Some fatten themselves up by eating as much as possible in the fall before winter or even during winter whenever they do find food.

From spring through autumn the Red Fox eats fruits and insects. But those two foods are not readily available in the winter. To survive, the fox changes its diet and eats small rodents.

Staying warm can be a problem even for mammals. Although mammals' fur has two layers of hair year-round, their winter coat is different. For some species, a winter coat is simply more hair (fur) than their summer coat. For others the winter hairs are actually thicker. Some grow longer hair. Some grow a coat of a different color. Some do it all.

This Eastern Gray Squirrel, a winter-adapted mammal, has two layers of fur. The outer layer has coarse, long hairs that protect the inner layer, or under hair. The under hair is shorter and finer. In winter, his coat gets thicker and helps him survive the cold.

Another way to stay warm is to stay under the snow. Snowflakes trap air and trapped air is good insulation. Some rodents, such as mice and voles, tunnel under the snow for the entire winter. Why not? A blanket of snow can even insulate plants for the winter.

...The Winter Warriors

S ome animals have developed several adaptations to survive the cold. One of my favorite survivors is a tiny bird called the Golden-crowned Kinglet. It winters in the woods across the northernmost United States and southern Canada, where the nighttime temperature can get to 30 degrees below zero.

Golden-crowned Kinglets are among the smallest birds in North America—only the size of hummingbirds (about 3.5 to 4 inches long). If you removed their feathers, their bodies would be the size of a cherry! So how do they survive the winter?

Golden-crowned Kinglets spend all day long eating up to three times their own weight in frozen moth caterpillars that they find in the trees. To keep warm at night, they fluff up their feathers and huddle together in groups of two or three to reduce the loss of body heat and they shiver to generate body heat.

Winter coats, changes in diet, living under the snow, shivering, and huddling are all adaptations that help animals to survive the winter. Can you think of any others?

Even with all their winter survival tactics, most Golden-crowned Kinglets don't make it through the winter. To keep their population going, survivors hatch as many as 22 chicks in two broods during the summer.

What's for Dinner?

Insects become dormant and many overwinter in trees: under the bark, on pine needles, even in buds. You can see birds looking for insects in trees every day.

Seeds are an important food for animals in the winter. Animals eat seeds from pine cones and also flowers such as Black-eyed Susans, Purple Coneflowers, and Sunflowers.

Berries. Some winter berry bushes produce berries that actually don't taste good to animals until after the berries have frozen and thawed. I guess that's nature's way of making sure that there will still be berries in the cold winter months.

Nuts, such as acorns from oak trees, are also an important food for deer, squirrels and even Blue Jays.

Agriculture. Many animals (for example, geese) have adapted to eat our crops and whatever is left over in fields during the winter.

Garbage some birds, such as crows and gulls, eat whatever and whenever they can. They will eat road kill and garbage, and even raid our trash cans. One day I saw a crow fly into a big dumpster and come out with a McDonald's bag in his beak. He put it on the ground, ripped it open, and had himself a few French Fries. Smart crow!

New Words?

Camouflage
(KAM-uh-flaj)

Coloring or patterns that help a predator to hide or blend in with its environment.

Let it Snow!

Here's a fun experiment to do during a snowfall. Put a piece of black construction paper in your freezer so it gets nice and cold. Then, take it outside and let the snow fall on it. You can see the individual snowflakes!

Who Cares? They Do!

The National Wildlife Federation (NWF) works to inspire Americans to protect wildlife for your future. At their website, you can become a member. Ask your parents if they would like to join. You can learn about nature and even symbolically adopt a Polar Bear, a Moose, or a Canada Lynx at their website, too. Learn more at:

www.nwf.org

Deer and ducks by Sophie Pan, age 7, of Boyds, MD.

Why would an animal turn white in the winter? *Camouflage*, of course! Predators need to be able to sneak up on their prey. Prey need to hide from predators. In winter, many trees and bushes are bare and the ground is covered with snow, leaving few hiding places. Being white against the snow is an advantage. If you're white, you can hide in plain sight. But hiding isn't the only advantage to being white. Another is insulation.

White fur and white plumage insulate better than dark fur or plumage. Really! Dark-colored fur and feathers have a dark pigment in them called melanin (MEL-uh-nin). White fur and feathers don't have melanin in them. White is actually the absence of color. The spaces left by the missing melanin in white fur and feathers create air pockets. Sunlight reflects from these air pockets making the fur or feathers look white.

The air pockets are good insulation, keeping white animals warmer than dark animals in cold weather. And in warm weather, the air pockets help to keep animals cool.

The Ptarmigan (top), Arctic Fox (middle) and Snowshoe Hare (right) all turn white in the winter. Being white is a huge advantage when you live in the snow.

Having feathers or fur that are full of air pockets has yet another advantage—*flotation* (flow-TAY-shun). Those air pockets created by the missing melanin also help an animal to float. Think of the Polar Bear swimming 40 miles through the Arctic Sea between floating blocks of ice. That's a long way to swim. The air pockets in its white fur help it to stay afloat. Polar bears are white year round and are always on the ice and snow in the Arctic. Air pockets in white feathers help to make birds float, too. Maybe that's why some birds, such as Snow Geese and Tundra Swans, are white year round.

You aren't likely to see a Polar Bear in your backyard. Depending on where you live, you might not see a Ptarmigan, or an Arctic Fox, or a Snowshoe Hare, either. But you might see the one winter white creature that I have in my backyard.

This species doesn't even show up until the first snowfall. I guess it likes being camouflaged in the snow. It sometimes stays just a day or so and leaves and then seems to magically return again the next time it snows. Its lack of fur or feathers makes it sensitive to sunlight. Sometimes I try to put a hat on its head but it never seems to stay on. It's actually an endangered species and it can't reproduce without the help of humans. So every time it snows I head out to welcome my friend, the snowman!

The snowman is an endangered species and it can't exist without our help. I hope you do your best to keep this winter tradition alive. Even the birds like snowmen! The Tufted Titmouse (left) is a species of bird that lives in my neighborhood all year long. The White-throated Sparrow (right) and the snowman are present only in the winter.

Winter Sleep

In winter, the birds have left, other animals have gone to sleep, and the rest endure the blistering cold. The leaves have gone, there is a soft blanket of snow on the ground, all is quiet, all is peaceful.

*By Zach Kelly, age 12,
Cherry Hill, NJ*

Snowflake Bentley

Do you know that no two snowflakes are alike? This discovery was made by Wilson A. Bentley, a farmer in Vermont. In 1885, he was the first person to photograph a single snowflake (also called snow crystals). During his life he photographed more than 5000 snowflakes and wrote a book about snowflakes. He became known as "Snowflake" Bentley. You might enjoy this book written about him:

Snowflake Bentley
by Jacqueline Briggs Martin
Houghton Mifflin, publisher.

Snowman in sunset by Abi Goeser, age 10, of Clive, IA.

Your Field Notes

This page is for your field notes. Field notes are a journal page where you record your outdoor observations—those you make "in the field". Your notes should include today's date and your location (such as your backyard). Write about the weather; the temperature, what the sky looks like, how the weather feels to you. You can also use this form to list the plants and animals you see or to write a story or poem about your winter nature walk. If you need additional pages, use blank paper or download free forms at our website, www.takeawalk.com. You can also use your Nature ID page (see page 26) to write about a specific plant or animal you observe.

Need more room to draw or write? Use blank paper or download free forms at www.takeawalk.com.

Draw a Map

Draw a map of the area you plan to explore: whether it's a park, your backyard or your schoolyard. Mark where you see birds or other animals and where you see tracks in the snow. Include some or all of these things:

Paths, sidewalks, buildings, and parking lots.

Trees or groups of trees and bushes. If you know what species they are, label them.

Bird feeders, birdhouses, and bird baths.

Flower or food gardens.

Wood piles.

Playground equipment.

Lakes, rivers, creeks, ponds, or swimming pools.

Each time you take a walk add more details to your map.

Need more room to draw or write? Use blank paper or download free forms at www.takeawalk.com.

15

Go! See What You Can See...

New Words?

Deciduous
(di-SID-jew-us)

Shedding leaves at the end of the growing season.

Remember that Nest!

If you find a nest, remember its location. Because birds are territorial, there's a good chance the bird will return to build again in the spring. You can be ready and watching for its return.

Field Guide to Bird Nests

If you like discovering bird nests you'll find this field guide helpful. See if your local library has a copy or ask for it at your favorite bookstore:

Peterson Field Guide: Eastern (or Western) Birds' Nests
by Hal. H. Harrison Briggs
Houghton Mifflin, publisher.

Keywords and Phrases

To learn more about trees and why they lose their leaves in the winter search for "deciduous" on the Web.

Snow scene by Jessica Ferber, age 8, of Cherry Hill, NJ

16

Observing nature in the winter is, in many ways, easier than any other time of year. You might not see the quantity of plants and animals that you could see in other seasons. But what's missing in nature can make it easier to see what's actually there. Animals are easier to see—they have fewer hiding places because **deciduous** trees and bushes lose their leaves. Animals are easier to see against the white snow (unless, of course, an animal is white). Animal tracks are easy to see in the snow.

So where should you start your nature observations? In bare trees and bushes, of course! And what should you look for? Nests! Look high and low in bushes and trees. Up high you might see squirrel nests or hornet nests. At different heights you can see bird nests. Some birds build nests low in bushes, giving you an opportunity to see a nest up close.

Most birds use their nests only during spring and summer, so most of the nests you see will be empty. But in some regions, the Great Horned Owl and the Bald Eagle begin nesting in the winter.

Squirrel nests, (top) high in trees, look like a wad of loose leaves. Bird nests (middle) are so easy to find in the winter and just as difficult to find in the summer when the leaves hide them. Great Horned Owls begin nesting as early as January. They might use an old Red-tailed Hawk nest or a cavity in a tree.

Look for birds. Many of the wintering birds are black, white, and/or gray. These colors help them to blend in with tree trunks. Take a minute to look over a tree carefully because it's possible that a bird could be above your head and, unless it's making noise, you wouldn't know it.

Listen for birds chirping and calling. Listen for woodpeckers trying to get at insects under the bark and Jays trying to crack open nuts and acorns.

Look for signs of birds too, like droppings on the ground. You might even find an owl pellet or two!

Also look on trees and bushes for signs of animals. Look for broken branches and stripped bark, signs that animals such as deer have been by. Look for scratches and marks on tree trunks created by raccoons going up and down to their homes.

One winter day Rob and I spotted a bird nest in a bare bush that had been covered over with hair and plant material. It was a curious sight. As we approached to observe it, suddenly a bazillion mice came jumping out (and I jumped out of my skin!) We backed off quickly so they could go back to their warm winter home. Mice in trees—who knew?

If you look closely you might find that bare trees aren't really bare at all!

Look in cracks in tree trunks. You might also find acorns stashed by squirrels or birds.

The White-footed mouse stays active in the winter. It stays warm inside its nest.

Don't Disturb Nests

Don't' remove or disturb a bird nest. Even if it's empty and even if you know the species of bird that built it will not reuse it. Why not? Well, it's illegal.

The Migratory Bird Treaty Act states that all migratory birds and their parts (including eggs, nests, and feathers) are protected and no one may own, remove, or disturb them. Canada, Japan, Mexico and Russia join the United States in protecting migratory birds.

In the United States, schools can apply for a permit that allows them to posses certain objects like feathers and empty nests for educational purposes. For more information about protection of migratory birds, search the Web for "Migratory Bird Act".

Whooooo's That Owl?

The owl on the corner of the pages in this book is a Snowy Owl.

Fox in snow by Emma Cain, age 11, of Moorestown, NJ.

Evergreen Tree

Evergreen trees are always green. With snow as a decoration. With good smelling pine and pricks. It is like no other tree and becomes so beautiful when Christmas time comes. It is a really nice tree for everyone.

By Roman Daniel, age 8, of Riverton, NJ

Thank goodness deer grow their own winter coats.

Trees that don't drop their leaves in winter are often called *evergreen* trees. They are always green. They drop their leaves like deciduous trees but not all at once. Leaves die and are replaced individually year-round.

Evergreen trees can have needle-leaf (pine and fir) scale-leaf (cedar) or broadleaf (holly) leaves.

In winter the evergreen trees are vital for the survival of wildlife. They provide food and shelter. Some animals eat needles from fir trees. Some birds eat the seeds from pinecones. Many birds eat the berries from evergreen trees.

Evergreens also offer good shelter. They are a place where birds can roost at night; and they do, often in large groups.

Some species of owls take cover in evergreens near the trunk of the tree, where they are well camouflaged.

When you are near evergreens, listen for birds. Look for signs of birds in evergreens by looking for their droppings (whitewash) on the ground or in the lower branches.

The Red Crossbill has a beak that is adapted to split open pinecones to get at the seed

This Long-eared Owl is perched next to the trunk of a pine tree. Do you think he looks like tree bark? I do!

One of my favorite evergreens is the Eastern Red Cedar. I like this species of tree because it always seems to be filled with birds in the winter. I also think it's interesting because its berries are not actually berries; they are cones with a fleshy covering. Everyone calls the cones berries—maybe because they don't know better, or maybe because they look like berries. I've always called them berries even though I know they're cones.

The berries of the Eastern Red Cedar start out green and turn light powder blue as they mature.

The Eastern Red Cedar grows in the Eastern U.S. and Canada. Many species of birds eat the berries (cones) and so do mice, deer, and game birds such as turkey and grouse. It's a common tree and its seeds are often spread by birds.

If you look along roadsides where telephone and electric wires run, you can sometimes see a row of Eastern Red Cedars growing right underneath the wires. They grow there because their seed is carried in the droppings of birds that perch on the wires.

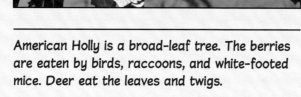

American Holly is a broad-leaf tree. The berries are eaten by birds, raccoons, and white-footed mice. Deer eat the leaves and twigs.

Another favorite evergreen of mine is the American Holly. It is the official state tree of Delaware. It grows berries in the winter that many animals eat, and it has become a symbol of winter and holidays. It is a popular holiday decoration and you can see it on cards, dishes, mugs and all kinds of things.

Antler Schmantler

White-tailed deer can cause damage to trees by rubbing their antlers on them. They seem to like young Red Cedars the most for this purpose. They rub their antlers to rub off the soft covering (called "velvet"). I guess it must be itchy. The bark of the tree gets stripped away by the rubbing.

Only males rub their antlers because only male deer, elk, and moose grow antlers. Not females. However, female caribou grow antlers when they are pregnant so they can use them as weapons when competing with the males for food. But they aren't really big weapons— female caribou antlers are only little points.

Male deer, elk, moose, and caribou grow antlers during the summer. Then they shed their antlers in the winter. Hunters call the discarded antlers "sheds".

Rodents chew on sheds because they are full of nutrients like calcium.

If you find sheds in the woods, it's okay to take them home with you.

You can tell the age of a male deer, elk, moose or caribou by the number of points on its antlers. Each year its antlers grow larger and grow one new point.

Dog

Cat

Mountain Lion (page 30)

American Mink (page 30)

Gray Wolf (page 30)

Red Fox (page 10)

Some animals can live in or near your backyard and go unseen by you, particularly those that are *nocturnal* (active at night). But animals leave tracks in mud and snow and tracking is a fun way to discover what is living in, passing through, or stopping by your yard. Looking at tracks is like looking at a guest list of wildlife in your neighborhood. When you see tracks, how do you identify which species made them? Here are some clues to look for:

Location: Consider your location and the species of animals that might be in your neighborhood. If you live in an eastern city, you can bet that the tracks you are looking at won't be from a mountain lion.

Size: Observe the size. Small animals make small tracks, of course!

Claws: Do the tracks include claw marks (triangular marks in front of the toe marks)? If so, they won't be from a cat, because cats retract their claws when they walk or run.

Animal tracks such as this Raccoon (top) and Coyote (bottom) are easy to see in newly-fallen snow.

Pattern: Check the pattern of the footprints. Are they in a straight line or did the animal roam around? Are the footprints neat and clean as if the animal were walking or is there a lot of broken snow around the tracks as if the animal were running? Write down your observations.

A field guide to animal tracks can help you if the tracks you see don't match any on these pages. One of my favorites is the **The Peterson Field Guide to Animal Tracks,** (Houghton Mifflin Publisher). It helps you to identify tracks and tells you about animal behavior. It even contains drawings of animal poop (called "scat" by the scientists). You can identify which animal the scat came from by its size and shape.

...Dog, Cat, Mouse, or Deer?

Tracks can be found in mud (frozen or wet) or in the snow, and each new snowfall turns your backyard into a guest list of wildlife. All you need to do is read the handwriting, oops, I mean paw-writing on the snow and mud. Here's a table to help you:

How many toes?	Which animal?
One	Horses, mules, donkeys, humans (wearing shoes or boots).
Two	Deer, elk, moose, sheep, goats, pigs, bison, caribou.
Three (or three plus one)	Birds (3 pointing forward and some birds have a fourth pointing to the back).
Four	Dogs (including pet dogs, wolves, coyotes and foxes), cats (including pet cats, bobcats, lynxes, and mountain lions) and rabbits.
Four front and five rear	Rodents (mice, rats, squirrels chipmunks, groundhogs, muskrats, porcupines).
Five	Raccoons, Humans (when barefoot, brrr!), weasels, badger, skunk, otter, mink, bears, beaver, opossum, wolverine, seals.
Six	I don't know and I don't want to find out. Aliens? Just kidding! There are no six toed creatures.

Raccoon (page 30)

Gray Squirrel (page 10)

Eastern Cottontail Rabbit (page 30)

Black Bear (page 6)

White-tailed Deer (cover and page 30)

American Robin (page 29)

Animal Tracks

I don't always see animals. Most of the time I see their tracks. I love to see the different tracks they make. You can tell where they have been and where they're going. It makes me connect with them. It makes me wonder why they went the paths they did.

By Chris Cline, age 13, of Shepherdsville, KY

Footprints in the Snow

When I step outside In the bright white snow I see all kinds of footprints From animals I know. There are prints from rabbits hopping Prints from frightened deer There are so many footprints In the snow out here

By Lorena Pohl, age 9, of Ames, IA.

Go! Make Maple Sugar...

The Take A Walk® Poem

Today I saw a big black bird fly
high up in the sky.
I walked into a garden where I
found a butterfly.
A squirrel was busy working as
he jumped from tree to tree.
Was I dreaming when I saw a
cloud smile back at me?

I felt the warm sun on my
face, I heard a robin sing.
I smelled the sweetness in the
air—I noticed everything!
Where were these things
before today? How could I
not have known?
Is this because I'm older now?
Is this because I've grown?

So much did I encounter that I
can't wait to learn more
About the things that I can
find just outside my door.
But the best part of my walk
today was my discovery—
That every time I take a walk,
I learn more about me!

By Jane Kirkland
With contributions by
Emily Heckman, age 9

Who Cares? They Do!

Sugar Maples and all trees
are important to our planet.
The Arbor Day Foundation
teaches people how to plant,
care for, and celebrate trees.
Learn more at:

www.arborday.org

We celebrate several holidays during the winter season. We follow many traditions, too. Do you have holiday traditions such as family dinners, giving gifts, and holiday decorations? Making maple syrup is a tradition for some families. It has a long history—early settlers learned how to make maple sugar from the Native Americans.

Maple sugar is made by collecting sap from—you guessed it—Sugar Maple trees. Sap is collected from February through March and the best sap comes from trees that are 40 years of age or older. A healthy sugar maple can produce sap for 100 years or more!

Warm days and freezing nights are the best weather conditions for producing sweet sap. Freezing temperatures at night cause carbon dioxide to make bubbles in the sap and help it to flow when it is heated by the sun during the day.

It takes a day to collect one gallon of sap (right, top and middle) and it takes 40 to 50 gallons of sap to produce one gallon of maple syrup. After the sap is collected it is boiled for a long time and stirred constantly to make the syrup (right).

To collect the tree sap, holes are tapped into the tree trunk. A spigot or tube is inserted into the holes and buckets are hung at the end of the tube or spigot. When the morning sun warms the tree it warms it first on the southeast side, making the sap drip from the tree, through the tube, and into the bucket. As the sun moves from east to west across the sky, other tap holes begin to flow. The sap can flow for just a few hours or for a few days.

As spring approaches and the tree blooms, the sap turns bitter and the sugaring season is over until the next year.

It's not easy to make maple sugaring your family tradition—you need mature trees, experience, and lots of equipment. But attending a maple sugar festival is a tradition you can start this year and continue for the rest of your life. It's such a sweet tradition!

Maple sugar festivals provide kids and their families the chance to experience sap collection (right, top). You can even make your own maple sugar taffy (right). YUM.

Where are the Festivals?

To find a maple sugar festival near you, ask your parents to check your local newspaper, or search for "Pennsylvania maple sugar festivals" (replacing "Pennsylvania" with your state or province).

Maple Sugaring

*Looking at the broken down trees
Seeing all the silent snow
In your fat-as-a-marshmallow snow clothes
Hearing banging, clanging sounds
Spile driller drilling
Hammers pounding
Cold as ice buckets
In your cold, creased hands
Laughing, chatting, working
Snow underfoot crunching
hanging sap buckets
A fantastic family chore*

By Mallory Carnes, age 11, of Fletcher, NC.

Spile

In Mallory's poem (above) she refers to a "spile". A spile is the name for the spout used to tap the maple sugar from the tree.

Take a Tree Walk

If you like learning about trees, you might like my book, **Take a Tree Walk**.

Learn More

Learn more about maple sugaring from the Vermont Maple Foundation at:

www.vermontmaple.org.

Snow

Snow is beautiful
Nothing has color
All is white but one small bird
Flying through the storm
Soon to see its family
Through the snow's beauty
Diamond coated plains and
fields
Darkness and silence
Snow topped trees and great
mountains
Even great cities
Are humbled by its beauty
Snow

By Adam Mohsen-Breen,
age 10, of Moorestown NJ.

Keywords and Phrases

To learn more about trees
and why they lose their leaves
in the winter search for
"migration" on the Web.

What's a Squirrel's favorite ballet?

The Nutcracker Suite!

Go! Play the Winter Version...

Every living thing needs water. We drink water. We bathe in water. And some animals live in water. Others, like waterfowl, breathe air and nest on land but spend much of their time on the water. Waterfowl are swimming birds such as ducks, geese, and swans.

Waterfowl have large feet and short legs to help them move through the water. Some geese and ducks eat grasses and other vegetation while on land. All waterfowl can eat while on the water. Some dive in the water for their food, eating fish or plants that grow in or on the water. Some waterfowl dabble—they tip their bodies forward to get at the food in the water but they don't actually put their entire body under the water like the diving ducks do. Only their heads go under the water and their butts go up in the air. I call that "Duck butting".

Ducks and geese are migrators. Most of them migrate south in winter and north in summer. Even so, they are well suited to living in cold, snowy climates. Most of the Canada Geese that live in Pennsylvania actually seem to have given up migration altogether. They are here all year round. When it's snowy here and ice covers our lake, there are still hundreds of them standing on the ice or paddling in the remaining open water. The cold doesn't seem to faze them at all.

Winter is a good time to observe waterfowl. But you'll probably need a pair of binoculars. The waterfowl will be in open water—and you'll need to observe them from the shore.

As you can see here, much of our lake freezes over but there is usually an area of deep water that remains open. It can get very crowded in our open water!

...Of Duck Duck Goose

When lakes and ponds freeze, waterfowl must move to open water—water that hasn't frozen. And open water is a great place to go birdwatching in the winter. The water in the lake where I live is deep. It is the deepest water for miles around. As a result, part of the lake stays open almost all year, even in very cold winters. That open water is like a bird magnet!

Ring-necked Ducks (top right) dive for their food. Mallards (middle right) are dabblers and so are Swans and Canada Geese (bottom right). Can you guess which animal made the tracks in the snow above? If you guessed "Canada Goose", you are correct!

Ice-skating Fox

In January our lake often freezes over. When it does, animals such as deer and fox can take a shortcut from one side of the lake to the other by traveling over the ice.

One winter, Dorothy Burke and I watched a Red Fox as he traveled across the ice back and forth every day. We could see him from my office in my home. We watched the fox for about a week. It was mating season for the foxes and we figured he must have been going to see his lady friend every day.

The fox would go from my yard across the lake every morning. He ran quickly across the ice, maybe because he was out in the open and afraid that he might be seen. As he ran across the ice he would sometimes slip and slide. It was funny to watch. Then, toward the end of the day, he would run back to my yard, slipping and sliding again.

One day, when he returned, he was followed by another Red Fox. We figured it was the female. After that day he never left our yard. That summer we saw the female and her kits (young foxes) in the meadow in our back yard.

Dorothy is an editor for Take a Walk® books; you can see her name on the title page of this book.

Field Guides

Nature Study Guild Publishers has a series of pocket sized field guides that are perfect to take on your winter nature walks.

They will help you to identify trees, plants, and tracks.

I own these four and I take them with me every time I take a nature winter walk:

Winter Tree Finder

Winter Weed Finder

Track Finder

Berry Finder

You can find the books at your local library, bookstore, or online at Amazon.com.

Here's an example of how to create a Nature ID Page. The facing page is a blank form for you to write down details about a plant or animal you see on your walk. You can draw it or take a photo of it and paste it on your form page. If it's a species you don't recognize, your notes will help you to identify the species when you research it in a field guide, at the library, or on the Web.

Date, Time, Weather Conditions: January 3, 3:00 PM. Very cold, maybe 20 degrees.

Habitat and location: We were supposed to go back to school today but we had 12 inches of snow yesterday. It took a long time to dig out our driveway and back door so we could go out to play in the snow. We were going to build a snowman but then we saw some tracks across our yard and we followed them. Then we saw a deer.

Size and physical description: It was brown and very tall and skinny.

Behavior Observation (if it is an animal): It was eating my Mom's rose bushes. I had to chase it away or she would get mad. Later, when I was back in the house I saw it again so I got some paint and I painted a picture of it while I was sitting at the kitchen table drinking hot chocolate.

Additional Notes: My Dad helped me to find the deer in a field guide.

Species Name: White-tailed Deer.

Deer by Morgan Sloan, age 12, of Moorestown, NJ.

...Nature ID Page of Your Own

Date, Time, Weather Conditions:

Habitat and location:

Size and physical description:

Behavior Observation (if it is an animal):

Additional Notes:

Species Name:

(Optional) Make a drawing or paste a photo here:

Need more room to draw or write? Use blank paper or download free forms at www.takeawalk.com.

More Winter Activities

You'll find some cool winter activities in this book, one of my favorites:

A Kid's Winter EcoJournal

By Toni Albert, Trickle Creek Books Publishers.

TrickleCreekBooks.com

Proverbs

A proverb is a short, ancient, popular saying. It is usually so old that no one knows the author. It might be a saying that is accepted as one of great wisdom. Or it might be a saying thought of as superstitious. Here are two winter proverbs:

Without having experienced the cold of winter, one cannot appreciate the warmth of spring.

-Chinese Proverb

There is no winter without snow, no spring without sunshine, and no happiness without companions.

-Korean Proverb

See also:

White-crowned Sparrow Song Sparrow House Sparrow (male) House Finch (male)

Purple Finch (male) Common Redpoll (female) American Tree Sparrow Pine Sisken (male)

American Goldfinch (winter) Downy Woodpecker (male) White-breasted Nuthatch Red-breasted Nuthatch

Eastern Towhee (male)

Evening Grosbeak (male)

Red-bellied Woodpecker (male)

Raven

Black-billed Magpie

Northern Flicker (female)

Carolina Wren

Sharp-shinned Hawk

Northern Cardinal (female)

Cowbird (male)

Black-capped Chickadee

Mourning Dove

European Starling

Stellar's Jay

Blue Jay

American Robin

See also:

White-tailed Deer

Mountain Lion

Coyote

American Mink

Gray Wolf

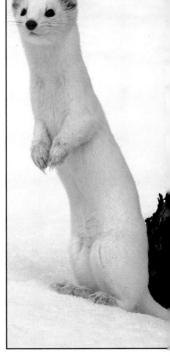

Long-tailed Weasel (winter)

Lynx

Moose

Eastern Cottontail

Raccoon

Go! Make a Difference

If you like observing nature, you might want to become a Citizen Scientist. That's a person who helps real scientists by gathering information and reporting it. Your family can choose from quite a few citizen scientist programs, including ones on birds, frogs, weather, plants, salamanders, butterflies and pigeons.

My favorite citizen scientist program is the Cornell Laboratory of Ornithology program called *Project FeederWatch*. In this program, you report the species of birds you see at your bird feeders from November through April. It only takes a few minutes a week to participate.

Sometimes when I take a winter walk I take along a bag of sunflower seed. I drop it on the snow, on fences, and on branches for the wild birds to find. I feel good knowing that, in some small way, I have helped them to survive another day.

You can observe your feeders from inside your house. It's not only fun and educational, the data provided by thousands of U.S. feeder watchers has helped scientists learn valuable information about our birds—where and when they migrate, their food preferences, information about their health and whether their population is growing or falling. Learn more about Project FeederWatch at **www.cornell.birds.edu.**

For Citizen Science programs in Canada, go to the Stewardship Canada Citizen Science website at **www.stewardshipcanada.ca.** On their home page, drop down the **Communities** menu and choose "Citizen Science."

In winter, I put up several bird feeders. Here, two Chipping Sparrows are enjoying the seed.

I hope you'll become a Citizen Scientist. It's an opportunity to learn a lot and help our planet at the same time!

Winter Nature Walk

I'm walking through the woods. It just snowed. I heard something. It's coming closer and closer. Then I see them. The deer. Three of them eating berries. Then they see me and leave, leaving footprints in the snow. I will remember that moment for the rest of my life.

By Liam Kelley, age 9, of Schwenksville, PA.

Signs of Spring

There's a point in every winter when we all get a little tired of the short, cold days and we start to think about spring. Here are some sure signs from nature that spring is on its way. Keep your eyes and ears open!

The smell of the earth and grass after a rainfall.

Spring peepers (tiny frogs) singing in the late afternoon and night. They sound like tiny bells jingling.

New buds growing on trees and flowers.

Woodpeckers drumming to attract mates.

Red-winged Blackbirds returning (usually the males return to claim territories before the females arrive).

Congratulations! Here you are at the end of the book. Now that you've discovered nature in the winter, can you see why I think it's exciting? I hope you saw animals and signs of animals that you never noticed before. Each time you take a winter nature walk you can see something different. Nature is always changing and there is so much more to the winter than sitting by a cozy fire, sledding down a hill, or building a snowman—although those are fun, too!

I hope that, as you learn more about nature and our environment, you'll find little ways in which you can make a difference to improve our planet. Just sharing this book with your friends and family can make a difference. Imagine if everyone in the world under-stood that nature needs our support year round and that it's exciting. Now **that** would make a difference.

You'll know winter is over when you see Crocus flowers poking through the snow. They are a true sign of spring!

When you don't have the time for a long winter walk or when it's just too cold to be outdoors, try taking a one-minute nature break. Or, as I prefer to say "Take a minute to be in it™". A minute is enough time to look around you to see which plants and animals are nearby. You can even take your nature break from in the house. Just look out the window to see what you can see. Try to take a nature break or a nature walk every day. It's good for your body, your mind, and your soul.

In case you've been wondering, yes, I see Bald Eagles every winter here at the lake. One year I saw three at one time! Some day, I hope a pair stays to nest. Can you imagine? I would be so excited to have Bald Eagles as neighbors.

Thank you for taking this walk with me. See you in the outdoors!

Photo Credits: photographs are copyrighted by the photographer or organization listed.

Alain | Dreamstime
Snowshoe Hare, page 12; Raccoon, page 30.

aleroy4 | Istock
Squirrel's nest, page 16.

Alisher, Duasbaew | Shutterstock
Common Redpoll, page 28.

Aunger, Mitch | Istock
American Holly, page 19.

Brenner, Matt | Istock
Sap bucket with spigot, page 22.

brm1949 | Istock
American Tree Sparrow, page 28; White-breasted Nuthatch, page 28.

Byland, Steve | Dreamstime
White-throated Sparrow and male Northern Cardinal, page 3; snowman with birds, page 13.

Campbell, Tony | Shutterstock
Eastern Gray Squirrel, page 10.

Canning, Ken | Dreamstime
Moose, page 30.

Chadwick, Sam | Shutterstock
Arctic Fox, page 12.

Cheever, Jason | Istock
Black-capped Chickadee, page 29.

cjmckendry | Istock
House Finch, page 28.

Claassen, David | Istock
An empty bird's nest, page 16.

Cronkhite, Jack | Shutterstock
Ptarmigan, page 12.

DeBoard, John | Shutterstock
Cottontail Rabbit, page 30.

Dodson, Rusty | Dreamstime
Garter snake, page 7.

Dotto, Lydia | Istock
Maple sugar taffy, page 23.

Dreamstime | Dreamstime
Northern Cardinal female, page 29; Gray Wolf, page 30.

Eastham, Bryan | Shutterstock
White-crowned Sparrow, page 28.

FloridaStock | Shutterstock
Mountain Lion, page 30.

foxtalbot | Istock
Covered sap buckets, page 22.

Garrenson, Katherine | Istock
White-footed Mouse, page 17.

Gleichman, Alan | Shutterstock
Great Horned Owl, page 16.

Gordo25 | Istock
Swan and Canada Goose, page 25.

Hebert, Daniel | Shutterstock
Downy Woodpecker, page 28.

Henke, Dieter | Istock
Syrup kettles, page 22.

Howard, Ronnie | Istock
Dark-eyed Junco, page 8.

Howard, Ronnie | Shutterstock
Long-tailed Weasel, winter coat, page 30.

Hunter, Brendan | Istock
Goose tracks in snow, page 25.

Jamsey | Istock
Northern Cardinal, page 1; Carolina Wren, page 29.

Joseph, Jemini | Shutterstock
Brown-headed Cowbird male, page 29.

Jurica, Jim | Shutterstock
Yellow-headed Blackbird, page 8.

Kehoe, Susan | Shutterstock
Black Bear, page 6.

Keifer, Cathy | Shutterstock
Red-bellied Woodpecker, page 29.

Kirkland, Jane and Rob | www.TakeAWalk.com
Snowy owl in the corner of every page; Eastern Bluebirds, page 9; Eastern Red Cedar berries, page 19; waterfowl at lake, page 24; Chipping Sparrows, page 31; Jane in the snow, page 31.

Krzysztof, Wiktor | Shutterstock
Prairie dog, page 6.

Kuchera, Geoffrey | Dreamstime
Coyote, page 30.

lightstalker | Istock
Purple Finch, page 28.

Linn, Willie | Shutterstock
Evening Grosbeak, page 29.

Lostlink | Dreamstime
European Starling, page 29; American Robin, page 29.

Loughlin, Kevin | www.WildsideNatureTours.com
Raccoon tracks in snow, page 20.

Macqueen, Bruce | Dreamstime
Song Sparrow, page 28; White-tailed Deer, page 30.

Matthew, Verena | Dreamstime
School buses, page 3.

McIninch | Istock
A family sugaring, page 23.

Mcwilliam, Steve | Dreamstime
Mallard Duck, page 25.

Missing35mm | Istock
Stellar's Jay, page 29.

Nialat | Shutterstock
American Mink, page 30.

Niche, Nature | Istock
Pine Sisken, page 28.

O'Dell, Lee | Shutterstock
Red Fox, page 10.

Outdoorsman | Dreamstime
Bald Eagle, page 2.

Pitcher, John | Istock
Long-eared Owl, page 18.

Proudlove, Hazel | Dreamstime
Crocus flower, page 32.

Renard-Wiart, Ben | Istock
Bald eagle, page 32.

RLHambley | Shutterstock
Blue Jay, page 29.

Robynrg | Shutterstock
Lynx, page 30.

Scheer, Alan | Shutterstock
Red-breasted Nuthatch, page 28.

Socrates | Dreamstime
House Sparrow, page 28.

sylvanworks | Istock
Chipmunk, page 7.

Tang, Gerald | www.TangsPhoto.com
Coyote tracks in snow, page 20.

Teekaygee | Dreamstime
Sharp-shinned Hawk, page 29.

Tessier, Paul | Istock
Snow Geese, page 9; Eastern Towhee, page 29.

TheDman | Istock
Mourning Dove, page 29.

Thompson, Michael J. | Shutterstock
Ring-necked Duck, page 25; Northern Flicker, page 29.

Tringali, JF | Istock
Acorns in tree, page 17.

Vandehey, Jason | Shutterstock
Red Crossbill, page 18.

Watkins, David | Shutterstock
Raven, page 29.

Woodruff, Michael | Dreamstime
Golden-crowned Kinglet, page 11.

Wrangler | Shutterstock
Black-billed Magpie, page 29.

"Take A Walk® Books are perfect for introducing young readers to our natural world!"
Jeff Corwin, Wildlife Biologist, Emmy-winning Executive Producer, and Host of Animal Planet's Popular TV Series, "The Jeff Corwin Experience".

"Nature in winter offers so much to the careful observer. Crisp air, quiet landscapes and a variety of bird and mammal activity. Pack this book in your day pack, put on your boots and coat and take your kids or students on a winter nature walk!"
Dr. Bernd Heinrich, Professor Emeritus of Biology at the University of Vermont and author of many books, including "The Winter World".

Take A Winter Nature Walk redefines the meaning of "snow day". Be the first among your friends to discover animal tracks, identify birds, and understand hibernation. This is your guide to exploring the fascinating world of nature in winter. Learn how animals adapt to survive harsh winters. Take field notes and record your observations. You'll be amazed at the numbers of species of plants and animals you can find in winter. Become a winter naturalist. Explore for a few minutes, an hour, or a day! When you Take A Walk® with us, we change the way you see our world!

This is a Take A Walk® book—part of the acclaimed, award-winning series of nature discovery books. Titles include:

Take a Backyard Bird Walk
Take a Tree Walk
Take a Walk With Butterflies and Dragonflies
Take a City Nature Walk
Take a Beach Walk
Take a Cloud Walk
Take a Wetlands Walk

Learn more at
www.TakeAWalk.com
www.NoStudentLeftIndoors.com
www.JaneKirkland.com

JNF051000 Juvenile Nonfiction/Science & Nature/General
EDU010000 Elementary Education
NAT000000 General Nature

For ages 8 and up
USA $9.95
Canada $10.95

Stillwater Publishing
PO Box 500
Lionville, PA, 19353
610-458-4000

NEW LEAF PAPER®
ENVIRONMENTAL BENEFITS STATEMENT
of using post-consumer waste fiber vs. virgin fiber

Stillwater Publishing saved the following resources by using New Leaf Reincarnation Matte, made with 50% post-consumer waste and processed chlorine free, and New Leaf Primavera Gloss, made with 60% post-consumer waste and elemental chlorine free. Both are manufactured with electricity that is offset with Green-e® certified renewable energy certificates.

trees	water	energy	solid waste	greenhouse gases
14 fully grown	3,837 gallons	6 million Btu	649 pounds	1,194 pounds

Calculations based on research by Environmental Defense Fund and other members of the Paper Task Force.

©2008 New Leaf Paper   www.newleafpaper.com

ANCIENT FOREST FRIENDLY™   NEW LEAF PAPER manufactured with wind power

ISBN: 978-0-9709754-7-8